QUESTIONS IN HISTORY

Series editor: Alan White

THE RISE OF ITALIAN FASCISM

Andrew Boxer

Collins Ed

To my wife, Sue.

Printed by Collins Educational
An imprint of HarperCollins*Publishers* Ltd
77–85 Fulham Palace Road
London W6 8JB

© HarperCollins*Publishers* Ltd 2000

First published 2000
10 9 8 7 6 5 4 3
ISBN 0 00 327123 4

Andrew Boxer asserts the moral right to be identified as the author of this work.

British Library Cataloguing in Publication Data
A catalogue record for this book is available from the British Library.

Acknowledgements

The author and publishers would like to thank the following for permission to reproduce illustrations:

Hulton Getty Picture Collection

Cover photograph: Mary Evans Picture Library

Edited by Lucy Nicholson
Designed by Derek Lee
Map by Tony Richardson
Production by Kathryn Botterill

Printed and bound in Singapore by Imago

www.**Collins**Education.com
On-line Support for Schools and Colleges

Contents

1 *Introduction*
Fascism in context

The birth of Fascism

On 23 March 1919 in a hall off the Piazza San Sepolcro in the northern industrial city of Milan, about 100 Italians met to form the *Fascio Italiano di Combattimento* (Italian Combat Group). They had been summoned by journalist Benito Mussolini through the pages of his newspaper *Il Popolo d'Italia* (The People of Italy). They were a motley bunch, with few constructive ideas, united mainly by their dislike of the existing political system.

Mussolini's Fascists did badly in the general election of November 1919. Not a single one was elected. But in October 1922, Mussolini was appointed prime minister. During the next four years he destroyed the constitution and made himself dictator. Such a spectacular rise could only happen in a country with considerable political, economic and social problems.

From unification to the First World War

Italy was not united until 1861, and in the following half-century little was done to tackle the country's divisions. When Italy joined the First World War in 1915 with grand ambitions to become a great European and imperial power, it was hampered by a political system that was not supported by the Italian people, and an economy gravely weakened by the growing disparity between conditions in the north and the south of the country.

The First World War and after

Participation in the First World War only worsened these problems and deepened the country's social and political divisions. Italy's middle-class liberal politicians were unable to cope with the country's difficult adjustment to peacetime conditions, and disillusionment with democratic, parliamentary government became widespread. Right-wing nationalists were angry that, despite being on the winning side, Italy had not gained enough from the peace settlement. Left-wing socialists exploited the country's economic problems and, in the 'red two years' of 1919–20, encouraged strikes and riots by the workers and peasants which succeeded in extracting important concessions from industrialists and landowners.

Support for Fascism grew rapidly as the property-owning classes, exasperated by the weakness of the government, turned in desperation to the only

Mussolini's love of show meant that a lioncub was a more than acceptable present from his henchman Aldo Finci. Its name was Ras.

movement that seemed capable of reversing the red tide of socialism. Even the liberal politicians in parliament, turning a blind eye to the violence of Fascist thugs, were keen to use Fascism to shore up their own power. The opponents of Fascism were too divided, weak and disorientated to offer any effective resistance. Influential conservative figures – the King, the Pope, leaders of the armed forces, wealthy industrialists and landowners – regarded Mussolini as the only man who could provide strong leadership and save Italy from the menace of socialism. In October 1922 Mussolini skilfully played on their fears of civil war by threatening to lead his Fascist squads in a march on Rome to seize power. The threat worked and Mussolini was appointed prime minister with the connivance of many of the country's democratic politicians and most of the conservative establishment.

The establishment of the Fascist dictatorship

Mussolini was able eventually to destroy the Italian constitution and make himself into a dictator because few Italians were prepared to stop him. Even when a major scandal erupted in 1924 which threatened his hold on power, most senior political figures expected someone other than themselves to take the lead in opposing him.

Opponents were intimidated by Fascist violence, liberals underestimated him or regarded their quarrels with rival parliamentary parties as more important, and too many conservative figures continued to regard socialism as more dangerous than Fascism. Nor did the Italian public have sufficient faith in their democracy to care much whether it survived or not. When, at the end of 1924, Mussolini was prodded into creating a dictatorship by pressure from his own Fascist lieutenants, he acted swiftly and snuffed out the last vestiges of democracy in the following two years.

2 Italy without Italians, 1861–1915

From unification to the First World War

Key points

◆ Italy before unification, 1815–70
◆ The legacy of unification
◆ Liberal Italy in decline
◆ Critics of liberal Italy
◆ The Giolitti era

Italy before unification, 1815–70

The Congress of Vienna, 1814–15

When the French emperor Napoleon was finally defeated in 1815, the states-men of Europe were already meeting in Vienna to redraw the continent's political and geographical map. The French Revolution and the Napoleonic era had frightened them, so they tried to restore Europe to the way it had been ruled in 1789. This meant that Italy remained divided into a number of different states that were either already part of the Austrian Empire or at least subject to its influence.

Lombardy and Venetia remained provinces of the Austrian Empire. Southern Italy and the island of Sicily were restored to the oppressive and corrupt rule of their Bourbon monarchy. The states of central Italy were ruled by princes or dukes, most of whom were related by marriage to the Austrian monarch. The Pope ruled a central swathe of territory, known as the Papal States, which includ-ed the city of Rome. Only the north-western state of Piedmont (which included the island of Sardinia) was independent of Austrian rule (see map, page 7).

The 1848 revolutions

By the middle of the century 'liberalism' (the belief that governments should be chosen from members of a parliament freely elected by citizens with wealth or property) became popular with the middle classes. Advocates of liberalism were also attracted to 'nationalism' (the belief that people with a common lan-guage, culture or racial heritage should live together separately from other nations). In 1848 most of Europe became engulfed in revolutions inspired by these two ideals. In Italy, the king of Piedmont tried to take advantage of the revolution in Vienna and kick the Austrians out of Lombardy and Venetia. Even

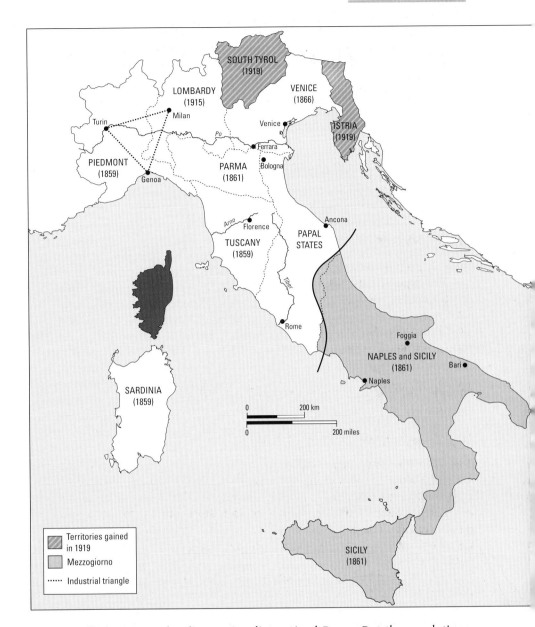

Italy in 1919

the Pope fled as excited Italian nationalists seized Rome. But the revolutions failed. An Austrian army crushed the Piedmontese, and French troops restored the Pope to Rome, remaining in the city for the next two decades to protect him.

Italian unification

In 1859 the Piedmontese tried once more to expel the Austrians from northern Italy. This time they had the support of the French, and succeeded in capturing Lombardy. Such success set in train a series of events that the Piedmontese struggled to control, and that ended in the unforeseen creation of a united Italy. Austrian weakness undermined the confidence of the rulers of the central Italian states whose political classes, fearful of revolutionary upheaval, voted for union with Piedmont.

In the south, a romantic revolutionary called Giuseppe Garibaldi, who dreamed of an Italy united by the efforts of the ordinary people, led a popular uprising which overthrew the monarchy. He marched on Rome, alarming politicians in Piedmont who wanted to extend their territory but were afraid of popular revolution. Garibaldi was eventually persuaded to hand his conquests over to Piedmont, and in 1861 the kingdom of Italy was proclaimed. In 1866 Venetia was added when Austria was defeated by the Prussians. Four years later, the French garrison in Rome was withdrawn to fight in the Franco-Prussian War and the Italian state gained control of Rome, which became its capital.

The legacy of unification

A contemporary remarked in 1861 that 'we have made Italy, now we must make Italians.' This was not an easy task. Only 2.5 per cent of the population used the Italian language; most spoke a regional dialect. Almost 70 per cent of Italians were illiterate, and in the poorer regions the rate was nearer 85 per cent. Italy's geography was also an obstacle to genuine unity (see map, page 7). The backwardness, conservatism and poverty of the south contrasted sharply with the relative sophistication and prosperity of the north.

Finally, the violent way in which unity had been achieved between 1859 and 1870 made the job of creating a single, united nation all the harder. The seizure of the Papal States had angered the Pope and made the Catholic Church a permanent enemy of the Italian state. Describing himself as a 'prisoner in the Vatican', Pope Pius IX told Catholics in 1871 that they should neither vote nor stand as candidates in parliamentary elections. This made it difficult for devout Catholics to accept the new state, and prevented the growth of a conservative political party in parliament. The attitude of the Papacy mellowed a little in the 1890s, but the ban on political activity by Catholics was not formally lifted until 1918.

The politics of liberal Italy

In 1880 Italy had an electorate of about 600,000; just over 2 per cent of the population. This meant that Italian politicians came almost exclusively from a prosperous elite of middle-class, professional people. Most of them were liberals who believed in parliamentary government, so long as it was dominated by men of their own class, and genuinely wanted to create a nation-state. They believed that economic progress, wider educational opportunities and pride in the nation's achievements would help to overcome Italy's divisions and backwardness.

The political system was modelled on that of Britain: the king appointed a prime minister, who needed support in the Chamber of Deputies to govern. However, there were no established political parties, so governments were loose coalitions made up of parliamentary factions. Parliament, as modern historian Martin Clark explains, was 'the arena where political favours were traded. Deputies were elected in order to advocate their constituents' interests to the central administration in Rome. If a deputy failed to put pressure on a minister, he risked losing votes back home; if a minister refused a deputy's request, the government risked losing the deputy's vote in parliament. But in a world of scarce resources requests sometimes had to be refused. So deputies' allegiances were temporary, and governments were unstable.'

This confusion extended to provincial and local government as well. In theory central government exercised considerable power over the localities.

There were 69 provinces, each run by a prefect, appointed by the central government in Rome. Prefects enjoyed extensive influence at town and village level, but in many areas, it was the local landlord who ruled. The prefect interfered as little as possible, expecting political support at the next election in return. As the number of voters was so small, bribery, manipulation and even the coercion of voters dominated elections. At both central and local level, politics was more about mutual back-scratching among the elite than great issues of policy and principle.

Italian economic and social problems

The most serious obstacle to unity was the economic and social backwardness of the south. Suffering from the natural disadvantages of a hostile climate, poor soil, barren hillsides and malaria-infested valleys, the provinces south of the *Mezzogiorno* (see map, page 7) had advanced little, in economic terms, since medieval times. Most of the land was divided into large estates (*latifondi*) by absent landlords who were content to live off their rents. It was farmed by peasant tenants lacking either the capital or the skill to do more than scratch a subsistence-living from the soil. There was considerable unemployment: in 1881 there were more than a million landless peasants in the south surviving on seasonal labouring jobs or contributing to the growing numbers of Italians who emigrated.

Agriculture dominated the economy of the north as well. In 1871, 60 per cent of Italy's working population were involved in farming. However, Italian agriculture was inefficient and uneconomic; farming did not produce enough food to feed the population, and 40 per cent of annual produce was consumed by those who grew it. Italy's industries were located exclusively in the north. Textile production was geared to export, and heavy industry relied on state contracts for the production of ships and railways.

Liberal Italy in decline

By the end of the 1880s, 'liberal Italy' appeared to be making progress. Industrial output was growing; more Italians could read and write; suffrage had been extended for both national and local elections; and, by joining the Triple Alliance with Germany and Austria in 1882, Italy had claimed a place among the great powers of Europe. But the political and economic developments of the next twenty years threatened this progress and subjected the political system of the country to considerable strain.

Economic difficulties

During the 1880s, Italian producers were undercut by foreigners; for example grain from the USA and textiles from the Far East became cheaper than Italian produce. The government's response was to introduce tariffs in 1887, a measure which resulted in a tariff war damaging Italian exports. France, which bought 40 per cent of Italy's exports, was particularly affected. Whole areas of Italy were ruined, and the disaster caused a banking crisis and a financial scandal which tainted a number of leading politicians.

The first appearance of the fasci

In 1893 disgruntled peasants in Sicily, incensed by the economic conditions, formed themselves into leagues (*fasci*) which supported socialist ideas, including a demand for the break-up of the *latifondi*. There were strikes, riots and arson. The government responded with harsh action and in 1894 the *fasci* were banned. Sicily was placed under martial law and a thousand people were deported.

In 1898 there were riots in many Italian regions against the high cost of bread. The worst incident was in Milan, where more than 80 people were killed and over 450 wounded when the army savagely suppressed rioting. In the wake of the violence, the government banned political parties and organisations considered subversive – socialists, radicals and even some Catholic groups. Such clumsy attempts at repression, however, further alienated those who were already outside the political system.

Italian agriculture becomes more capitalist

Beginning in the 1870s and 1880s, schemes for land reclamation and drainage in the Po Valley (see map, page 7) introduced commercialised, capitalist farming to the region. Much of the newly-cultivated land was owned by companies who hired landless peasants (*braccianti*) or migrant labourers to work for them. These workers' living conditions were poor and their wages low.

This capitalist farming developed alongside the more traditional share-cropping system (common throughout central and northern Italy) by which large land-holdings were divided among a number of peasants (*obbligati*). The proprietor provided most of the capital and sold much of the produce. In return, the peasants received a share of the crop and enjoyed some security of tenure. This was a socially conservative system, offering no incentive to the peasants to do anything more than grow enough to feed their families. The crisis in Italian agriculture in the 1890s made landlords anxious to maximise their profits and sell more produce. To make their farms more profitable, they squeezed their tenants' share of the crop or forced them to provide more of the capital. Some threw *obbligati* off the land altogether. Such developments made northern Italian peasants, both *braccianti* and *obbligati*, more willing to support radical ideas like socialism.

Industrial development

In the mid-1890s Italian industry entered a decade of sustained economic growth. Iron and steel, shipbuilding, engineering, electricity, chemicals and vehicle production all expanded. This development occurred exclusively in the north and the Po Valley, especially in the 'industrial triangle' bordered by the cities of Milan, Genoa and Turin. Not only did it widen the growing gulf between the wealthy north and the impoverished south, it also created a powerful class of industrialists and bankers who expected the state to look after its interests. At the same time, a lower middle class of managers, bureaucrats and white-collar workers also emerged – educated, ambitious people willing to vote for parties that would challenge the closed world of liberal politics.

Industrialisation had a major impact on the towns and cities of northern Italy, which grew in size as migrants flocked in from the countryside. The population of Milan doubled between 1871 and 1911. In 1881 fewer than a quarter of Italians lived in towns with more than 20,000 inhabitants. By 1911 more than a third did.

Unfortunately, the cities were not equipped to cope with the influx and poor workers found themselves living in overcrowded, unsanitary conditions.

Urbanisation, the expansion of industry and the development of a modern capitalist economy all contributed to the growth and spread of a range of ideas that challenged the traditional values of Italy's liberal ruling elite and their hold on power. The most important of these new ideas were socialism, syndicalism and futurism.

Critics of liberal Italy

● Socialism

In 1891 a Milanese lawyer, Filippo Turati, tried to bring together Italy's social-ist groups into a single party. He was only partially successful – a year later, at their congress in Genoa, the socialists split. Most followed Turati and adopted a moderate programme aiming, in the short term, at gaining improvements in workers' pay and conditions and, in the long term, at creat-ing a socialist state. A smaller group followed an anarchist line, believing that socialists should not participate in elections. Turati's group survived the government repression of the 1890s. In 1895, meeting in secret, it was renamed the Italian Socialist Party (PSI). In 1896 the party was publishing its own daily newspaper, called *Avanti!* (Forward!) and in the general election of 1900 the party won 32 seats. However, its deputies were almost exclusively middle-class intellectuals – workers and peasants wanting to participate in politics joined the rapidly-expanding trade unions or the Chambers of Labour.

By 1902 nearly 250,000 industrial workers had joined socialist unions, which pressed for higher wages and organised strikes. The unions were dominated by skilled male workers; unskilled workers and women were not organised enough, nor able to exert any industrial muscle. More popular than the unions were the Chambers of Labour, which first sprang up in the 1890s. They were self-help organisations that ran schools, labour exchanges, shops and housing co-operatives. Their socialism was based more on Christian morality than on Marxist ideology. The Chambers of Labour help to explain why Italian peasants, unlike peasants anywhere else in the industrialised world, were recruited to socialism.

● Syndicalism

Some workers and middle-class intellectuals were drawn to syndicalism, a movement which originated in France. Syndicalists believed that workers should seize control of their factories by force and form syndicates, initially to establish workers' control of industry, and then to take power in the state. They despised the moderate socialism of men such as Turati as a betrayal of the true interests of the working class.

By 1914 the *Unione Sindacale Italiana* (USI) had about 100,000 members. It added nationalism to the left-wing economic ideas of the original syndicalists: members believed that national unity was essential to the modernisation of Italy and that Italian imperialism was crucial to the spread of their ideas abroad. In addition, the syndicalists believed that actions, slogans, symbols and rallies would have more impact on the masses than reasoned argument.

● **Futurism**

Futurists hated the comfortable, complacent, cosy life of middle-class, bourgeois society. Their manifesto of 1909 declared: 'Courage, rashness and rebellion are the elements of our poetry … we glorify war – the only cure for the world – militarism and patriotism … the beautiful ideas that kill.' They believed that Italy's conservative values, in art, music and literature as well as politics, ought to be swept away by violence and war. Only then would Italy be restored to greatness. Their leader, Filippo Marinetti, was one of Mussolini's earliest supporters.

Irredentism and Empire

It was not just the Syndicalists and the Futurists who wanted Italy to assert itself abroad. Many of the more conservative members of the liberal elite wanted Italy to become one of the great European powers. They believed that Italy should reclaim the 'unredeemed lands' (*terre irredente*) of Trentino and Trieste, where large numbers of Italians were still living under Austrian rule. They also wanted an overseas empire which, they believed, would cement national pride and bring tangible economic benefits.

In the 1880s, as the major powers of Europe carved up Africa between them, Italian nationalists clamoured for Italy to have her share, particularly in North Africa. A year after the French seized Tunis in 1881 (where there were 9,000 Italian settlers and just 200 Frenchmen), the Italian government signed an alliance with France's European rivals, Germany and Austria. But the strength of irredentist feeling against the Austrian Empire meant that Italy was always an uneasy member of the Triple Alliance.

In 1885, Italy acquired the port of Massawa, on the Red Sea. In the following years, the Italians pushed further inland into Eritrea and Somalia, towards the independent kingdom of Abyssinia. In March 1896, however, they were decisively beaten by the Abyssinian army at the Battle of Adowa. More than 5,000 Italians were killed and nearly 2,000 taken prisoner. It was the first time a European power had been defeated by 'savage' Africans and a devastating blow to Italian prestige. Many Italian nationalists blamed the country's international weakness on Italy's 'corrupt' liberal system.

The Giolitti era

The politics of trasformismo

In October 1876 the newly-appointed Italian prime minister, Agostino Depretis, said that his aim was 'to bring about the fertile transformation of parties, the unification of all shades of liberal in parliament.' This became known as *trasformismo* – bringing together moderate elements from a range of parties and ideas in a government of national unity. To its critics, however, it was just another cynical ploy by which self-serving politicians hoped to manage the parliamentary factions and cling onto power.

It was Giovanni Giolitti, the dominant Italian politician from 1900 until the outbreak of the First World War, who tried to perfect the politics of *trasformismo*. He was aware that Italian politics needed to adapt to the challenges posed by rapid economic development and the emergence of socialism. When he became prime minister for the second time in 1903 he set out to appeal to

Giovanni Giolitti, advocate of the politics of *trasformismo* and the 'face' of liberal Italy.

moderate socialists and Catholics in a bid to bring out-siders into the political system and strengthen the Italian state. It was *trasformismo* on a grand scale.

Giolitti's policies

Giolitti's government enacted progressive social reforms and won moderate socialist support by adopting a neutral stance in labour disputes. The Catholic Church, regarding socialism as far worse than liberalism, was prepared to be flexible: Catholics were permitted to vote in constituencies where otherwise a socialist might get elected. In the 1909 election more than 40 Catholics even stood as parliamentary candidates, and 17 of them were elected.

In 1912 Giolitti's government granted the vote to vir-tually all adult men, increasing the electorate from under three million to nearly eight and a half million. Since five million of the new voters were illiterate, it was assumed that the electorate could be managed in the same way. But the 1913 election brought an increase in the number of socialist and Catholic Deputies, and Giolitti found it increasingly hard to pursue policies acceptable to both.

The Libyan War, 1911–12

In September 1911 Italy invaded Libya. There were fears that growing French power might squeeze Italy out of north Africa, and Giolitti knew that he had to placate nationalist opinion. Militarily, the war was relatively successful – the Turkish Empire handed Libya over to Italy in October 1912. Unfortunately for Giolitti, it also polarised opinion in Italy and destroyed his attempts at *trasformismo*. The socialists, who disliked imperialism on principle, abandoned their support for Giolitti's liberal government. The more radical faction of the Socialist Party, which had never liked co-operating with Giolitti, gained control of the PSI. The new editor of the Party newspaper *Avanti!* was an excitable young revolutionary called Benito Mussolini: his articles denounced the war, militarism and Italy's corrupt parliamentary system.

Although nationalists were pleased by the war, they did not become support-ers of Giolitti. Instead, they loudly denounced socialists as unpatriotic, blaming Giolitti's earlier conciliatory policies (such as that of neutrality towards strikers) for allowing left-wing ideas to flourish. Nationalists also attacked *trasformismo* as corrupt and claimed that an authoritarian government was needed if Italy was to become a truly great power.

Red Week, 1914

In March 1914 Giolitti's parliamentary coalition broke up and he resigned, but nothing demonstrated the failure of his *trasformismo* policies more than the events of Red Week in June 1914. When three workers were killed by police trying to control an anti-militarist demonstration in the port of Ancona, the

Socialist Party called for a general strike. The response was so violent and widespread that trade union leaders and the authorities lost control. In one small town the workers proclaimed a republic, and in Ravenna peasants captured an army general and six officers. The spontaneity and extent of the violence worried moderate trade union leaders, who called off the strike after two days, and the army was able to restore law and order.

Red Week had important consequences. Property owners were alarmed by the threat from the left. The socialists were more bitterly divided than before between the revolutionaries and the moderates; each blamed the other for the failure of Red Week. *Trasformismo* seemed a hopelessly inadequate tool for reconciling the divisions in Italian society.

Studying Italy without Italians

1 Which posed the greater threat to the stability of Italy between 1880 and 1914, the left or the right? Consider the following points:

a) The Left   the violence of the 1890s
              the importance of industrialisation
              the growth of socialism
              divisions between revolutionaries and moderates
              Red Week

b) The Right   the attitude of the Roman Catholic Church
              the strength of nationalist feelings: irredentism and
              imperialism
              disillusionment with the parliamentary system

2 Both Syndicalism and Futurism contained a mixture of ideas, some of which are normally associated with the left and others with the right. In two separate columns, list the left-wing and the right-wing ideas of each of the two movements.

3 What were the most important reasons preventing Giolitti from stabilising Italian politics? Expand on each of the following points and place them in order of importance:

a) the legacy of disunity before 1861
b) the north-south divide in Italy
c) the impact of Italy's capitalist development: industry and modernisation
d) the growth and strength of groups hostile to the liberal system:
      socialism, futurism, syndicalism
e) the strength of nationalist and imperialist feelings
f) the domestic impact of the Libyan War

3 The growth of discontent, 1915–1920

The First World War and its aftermath

Key points

- Italy's intervention in the war
- The domestic impact of the war
- The mutilated victory
- Post-war political developments
- The *biennio rosso* in the cities
- The *biennio rosso* in the countryside

Italy's intervention in the war

Attitudes towards intervention

When the First World War broke out in the summer of 1914, Italy remained neutral. Few Italians had much sympathy with their allies in the Triple Alliance, because they were fearful of Austrian ambitions in the Balkans and resented Austrian rule over Trentino and Trieste. There was, however, an assorted, noisy minority, of all shades of political opinion, who believed that Italy should fight on the side of Britain and France.

Among the interventionists, the left sympathised with Britain and France against German militarism, and some hoped that war would bring revolution to Italy. The nationalists on the right argued that only by joining the western powers against Austria could Italy make territorial gains. The Socialist Party condemned the war as a squabble between capitalists for additional markets from which the working class would gain nothing. Catholics disliked the idea of fighting against Catholic Austria, and Giolitti's liberal supporters argued that Italy could use her neutrality to extract concessions from Austria.

The decision to join the war

Prime minister Antonio Salandra was influenced by irredentism. In September 1914, he told a colleague that 'I cannot hesitate: if I thought I had had the opportunity to restore Trentino and Trieste to Italy and that I had let it slip, I would not have a moment's peace for the rest of my life.' He decided to bargain with both sides to see what they would offer for Italian support. The Entente powers won and in April 1915 Italy signed the Treaty of London committing the country to war on the side of Britain and France. The Treaty secretly promised Italy considerable gains: Trentino, Trieste, the South Tyrol, Istria and part of Dalmatia.

Because the Treaty was secret, deputies in parliament spent most of May 1915 arguing about neutrality and intervention, accompanied by noisy street demonstrations in favour of war, organised by nationalists and the *fasci di azione rivoluzionaria* (revolutionary action groups). This gave rise to the myth that Italy had joined the war because belligerent action by demonstrators had forced the decision on a weak and indecisive parliament.

Italy in the war: Caporetto and its consequences

The Italo-Austrian front rapidly became a stalemate, with large conscript armies engaged in a sterile slogging match. Morale in the Italian army was low. Pay, conditions, supplies and entertainment were poor. In the words of historian Martin Clark, the Italian army was 'sullen, often illiterate, ill-equipped … torn away from its homes and fields to fight on foreign soil for incomprehensible reasons'. Discipline was harsh and the desertion rate high.

In October 1917 the Italian army was decisively defeated by the Austrians at the Battle of Caporetto. More than 10,000 Italians were killed, 300,000 wounded and a further 300,000 captured. The Austrians advanced 70 miles into Italy itself. Although Caporetto was a shock, the need to defend Italian soil and the reforms of the new commander-in-chief improved morale. One innovation was the creation of *arditi* – specially-trained commandos whose job was to carry out dangerous, heroic and highly publicised missions. After the war many of these men, unable to adjust to civilian life, became early recruits to Fascism. By the autumn of 1918, with both the German and the Austrian armies collapsing, the Italians were able to expel the Austrians and proclaim a victory at Vittorio Veneto. The Italian army occupied Trentino and Trieste in November.

The domestic impact of the war

Industry and agriculture

Italian industry, especially in the Milan-Turin-Genoa triangle, expanded rapidly during the war to meet the government's demand for munitions which, together with the soldiers' wages, pension payments and food subsidies, threw the nation's budget into deficit. The gap was bridged by borrowing and by printing money, solutions that resulted in inflation. Wholesale prices rose by more than 400 per cent between 1913 and 1918.

The industrial labour force grew to keep up with this expansion, especially in the northern cities. But prices rose faster than wages and the workers were subject to strict wartime discipline, so the cities became centres of potential discontent. In August 1917 there were bread riots in Turin, suppressed by the army at the cost of 50 lives. Despite their economic hardship, the industrial workers were regarded as *imboscati* (shirkers) by the front-line soldiers, of whom a disproportionate number were peasants, mostly conscripted from the south. The soldiers' pay and conditions were much worse than those of the workers. The tensions between workers and soldiers were to have important repercussions after the war.

Agriculture was affected more positively; although the countryside lost millions of men to the army, the production of food was not adversely affected.

Conscription soaked up some of the rural unemployed, and agricultural production was maintained by women, children and old people. Wartime inflation reduced or wiped out many debts, and some peasants became prosperous for the first time in their lives. This created a demand for land that was fuelled by government propaganda promising its peasant soldiers their own land after the war. The war was planting the seeds of a rural revolution.

Politics

The war widened existing political divisions. Liberals could not agree on whether Italy was fighting a war of liberation from Austrian oppression or (once the Bolsheviks in Russia had published the terms of the secret Treaty of London) a war of conquest. Catholics were mostly patriotic but Pope Benedict XV refused to support the war and denounced it in August 1917 as 'useless slaughter'. The split in socialist ranks also widened: revolutionary socialists were implacable in their hostility to the war, but moderate socialists, though they disliked it, regarded it as a patriotic cause. Nationalists were angered by Italy's lack of success, which they blamed on the spread of socialism and the weakness of the parliamentary system.

The mutilated victory

The Italian prime minister, Vittorio Emanuele Orlando, attended the post-war peace conference at Versailles as leader of one of the victorious powers. He demanded the territories that had been promised at the Treaty of London, and most were granted. President Wilson of the USA, who had not signed the Treaty of London and who wanted the principle of nationality respected in decisions about disputed territories, would not allow the Italians to have the Dalmatian coast. Nor would he permit them to take Fiume (which had not been mentioned in the London treaty) even though the population of the town was largely Italian-speaking. Fiume was to be a free city. The Italian delegation left Versailles in disgust when they were also denied a share of Germany's African colonies. The poet Gabriele D'Annunzio summed up nationalist anger over the Versailles Settlement when he called it Italy's 'mutilated victory'.

The seizure of Fiume

In September 1919 D'Annunzio, leading a motley gang of about 2,000 nationalists and former *arditi*, seized Fiume. The Italian prime minister, Francesco Nitti, felt he could neither support D'Annunzio for fear of alienating the great powers, nor expel him because of his popularity in Italy. D'Annunzio's regime in Fiume lasted for just over a year. When Giolitti returned as prime minister in June 1920 he negotiated a settlement with Yugoslavia by which Fiume would remain an independent city. In December 1920, when Giolitti ordered the Italian navy to blockade Fiume and expel D'Annunzio, the poet's forces melted away rapidly, content that they had kept Fiume out of Yugoslav hands.

The episode should be noted because D'Annunzio's methods and style were later to be copied by the Fascists. He had carried out a daring adventure in defiance of conventional rules; his actions seemed to show that decisive acts of force were more effective than parliamentary talk. His brutal treatment of opponents, his flair for self-advertisement and his flamboyant emphasis on parades, uniforms and regular public acclamation, were all developed by Mussolini and his Fascists.

Post-war political developments

The formation of the Popular Party

In 1918 the Pope formally lifted the ban on Catholic political activity. This was followed by the formation of a Catholic party in 1919. The *Partito Popolare Italiano* (PPI) was sanctioned by the Pope and led by a priest, Luigi Sturzo, but it did not wish to be the political voice of the Vatican. It remained a secular party aiming to win the support of devout Italians and preserve them from the perils of socialism. Many of its members supported the peasants in their efforts to secure land.

Socialist radicalism

The revolutionary faction had come to dominate the leadership of the PSI during the war. Partly inspired by the success of the Bolsheviks in Russia, their propaganda demanded immediate revolution and a dictatorship of the proletariat. In August 1919 a socialist manifesto proclaimed that 'the proletariat must be incited to the violent seizure of political and economic power, and this must be handed over entirely and exclusively to the Workers' and Peasants' Council'. However, the leaders of the party were less ruthless than their rhetoric and were divided about how to exploit the post-war unrest in Italy. Many of them were out of touch with events in the provinces, where the successes of the 'red two years' were achieved in the countryside by unions and Chambers of Labour, and in the cities by factory councils inspired as much by syndicalism as by socialism. However, the revolutionary posturing of the party's parliamentary leaders prevented them from taking part in any liberal coalition governments.

Government instability

Two important constitutional changes contributed to the growing instability of Italian parliamentary politics:

◆ **December 1918**: the government gave the vote to all men in order to reward those who had fought in the war;

◆ **August 1919**: proportional representation was introduced.

In the first elections held under the new rules in November 1919, the PSI and the PPI became the two largest parties. The liberals were reduced to a few bickering factions, and it became increasingly difficult to form governing coalitions. The election of May 1921 confirmed this pattern: between June 1919 and Mussolini's appointment in October 1922, there were four different prime ministers.

The biennio rosso *in the cities*

Post-war industrial problems

Once the government contracts for wartime munitions ended, many Italian industries found themselves without markets. There was no domestic demand for such goods, nor could they be exported because foreign governments were also cutting back their expenditure on armaments. Bankruptcies and unemployment followed, the latter worsened by the demobilisation of the army. By November 1919 there were two million unemployed in Italy.

Inflation

Inflation continued, reducing pensions, savings and the incomes of those who lived from renting their property. Many middle-class Italians, especially those who had invested their savings in war bonds and lost relatives in the war, were especially bitter. They resented both the industrialists who had made big profits from war contracts and the workers whom they regarded as *imboscati*. The workers, however, were suffering too, because inflation reduced the purchasing power of their wages. The unemployed were even worse off.

Labour unrest and militancy

The result of these difficulties was labour unrest on an unprecedented scale. Because the strict wartime discipline had ended, workers were free to join unions, whose membership expanded rapidly. Between 1918 and the end of 1920, membership of socialist trade unions rose from 250,000 to 2,000,000. Some socialist political and trade union leaders believed that the Bolshevik Revolution in Russia was about to be copied in Italy.

In the summer of 1919 a rise in food prices provoked riots in central and northern Italy. Shops were looted and granaries raided. The government, instead of suppressing the violence with force, ordered the prefects to co-operate with local Chambers of Labour in requisitioning grain supplies and holding down prices. The Socialists, who blamed the price rises on greedy shopkeepers, gloated over their victory. One socialist newspaper declared that 'we shall not move a finger, nor say a word, to prevent the starvers of the people from being strung from the lamp-posts'. The government's decision ended the violence, but angered traders and shopkeepers, who felt that the government was being weak and failing to protect them.

The government also backed down when faced with problems in the factories. When workers occupied the Mazzoni factory in Pinerolo because the owner refused their wage demands, the government appointed one of its officials as provisional director of the factory. Other factory owners and industrialists responded to the strikes by granting wage increases. More than a million workers went on strike in 1919; many of the strikes were accompanied by violent rioting or the occupation of factories by the workers.

The growth of unrest

In April 1920 there was a ten-day general strike in Piedmont, and in June some army units stationed in Ancona mutinied against being transferred to Albania. In an echo of 'Red Week', they were supported by the workers of the region. The unrest reached its climax in September when more than 400,000 workers in the industrial cities of the north occupied their factories to prevent a lock-out by the owners. It looked like the start of Italy's proletariat revolution. The prime minister (Giolitti, once again) refused to use force against the workers in case it provoked worse trouble, and calculated that the occupation would end once the workers discovered that they could not run the factories without raw materials and customers. The occupation lasted for eight weeks and fizzled out when the government brokered a compromise by which unions would be offered a role in management. Once again, however, the government had appeared weak in the face of aggressive socialism.

Labour militancy receded in 1921 as Italy was hit by an economic slump that undermined the effectiveness of striking. But the unrest did have lasting consequences. The socialists lost confidence because the proletarian revolution had failed to materialise. The property-owning classes, angered by the concessions forced out of them, were dismayed by what they saw as the government's weak handling of the trouble, and disillusioned with democratic parliamentary government, which seemed more interested in appeasing socialism than in upholding law and order.

The biennio rosso *in the countryside*

Transfer of land in the south

The *biennio rosso* was as turbulent in the Italian countryside as it was in the towns. Conscripted peasants returned from the war expecting to have their demands for land satisfied. There was plenty of uncultivated land in the south, much of it on the *latifondi*. Many peasant soldiers joined ex-servicemen's associations which, with the support of Catholic peasant leagues, sponsored and organised an occupation of the land. About a million hectares passed into peasant ownership, often in the form of peasant co-operatives that rented or leased the land from the former owners. Many *latifondi* entirely disappeared.

However, the transfer of land was a deeply conservative event. The socialists, who had little support in the south (except in Apulia), played only a small part in it. Once the peasants had acquired their land, they had no further interest in change and reinforced the conservative social structure of the area. There was much more trouble in central and northern Italy.

Peasant discontent in central and northern Italy

At the end of the 19th century, agriculture north of the *Mezzogiorno* had become more commercialised and peasants were ready to support revolutionary ideas. The *braccianti* joined socialist leagues and supported the revolutionary faction within the PSI. By 1920 the socialist agricultural federation (*Federterra*) had 900,000 members, recruited from the *braccianti* and the disgruntled *obbligati* of central Italy. However, the majority of tenant farmers and share-croppers joined the Catholic Peasants League which, by 1920, had 1,250,000 members.

Militant agricultural workers soon demonstrated their power. In Ferrara, a strike lasting just twelve days in February and March 1920 succeeded in forcing the capitulation of the landowners. Wage rises were granted, proprietors agreed to recruit only unionised labour and the Chambers of Labour were to determine how many workers were needed. One socialist leader in the region boasted that this agreement was the prelude to 'the control and possession of the land by those who work it'. This success was followed in July 1920 by a massive strike of over 500,000 share-croppers in Tuscany. The landlords were forced to concede that more than 50 per cent of profit would go to the tenants, who would also enjoy security of tenure, while the owners were to bear a higher proportion of the costs. Landowners capitulated easily because they knew that, like the industrialists, they would get no support from central government if they resisted. They were also intimidated by violence, although this was later exaggerated by the Fascists to justify their own violence against the left.

Fascism – the only option?

In the autumn of 1920 the socialists made big gains in the local elections. This further alarmed Italy's property-owning classes, who saw the red flag flying from their local town hall and feared that they would face higher taxes to pay for public works controlled by socialist unions. As the slump reduced their incomes, and the government in Rome seemed too weak to resist the red tide, they turned in desperation to the only movement that seemed willing and able to fight back: Mussolini's Fascists.

And yet, ironically, the socialists were to become victims of their own success, which exposed the weaknesses and divisions of their movement. How should they exploit and consolidate the gains they had made? Should they be content with better pay and conditions for working people, or take control of the machinery of state? Were local councils and factory committees powerful enough to usher in a revolution? Was the Socialist Party sufficiently well-led and organised to exploit and control the situation? It was partly because so few socialists faced up to these questions or knew the answers to them that their response to the Fascist counter-attack in 1921 was so feeble.

Studying the growth of discontent in Italy 1915–1920

1   What problems might the Italian government have faced if it had *not* joined the war in 1915? Consider the following points:
a) the strength of irredentist feeling in Italy
b) increasing reliance on the Socialists and Catholics in parliament
c) the possibility of Italian claims being ignored at the Versailles Conference

2   The German statesman Bismarck once remarked that 'Italy has a large appetite, but poor teeth'. To what extent did Italy's experience in the First World War show that he was right? Consider the following points:
a) Italy's economic and political weaknesses in 1915
b) claims for territory made by Italian nationalists before and after the war
c) the quality of Italy's army
d) the economic and political difficulties caused by the war

3   Why do you think the response of the Italian government to the *biennio rosso* was so feeble? Consider the following points:
a) the politics of *trasformismo*: attempts to win over moderate socialism
b) fears of a bloodbath
c) worries about the Russian Revolution

4   Why did Italy's left-wing groups fail to turn the *biennio rosso* into a socialist revolution? Consider the following points:
a) how united were the left?
b) how effective was the national leadership of the Socialist Party?
c) were they expecting help from the Bolsheviks in Russia?
d) did the workers and peasants want a socialist revolution or just better pay and conditions?
e) did their success help to provoke a violent counter-revolution from the right?

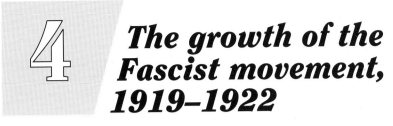

4 The growth of the Fascist movement, 1919–1922

Mussolini and the Fascist Party

Key points

◆ Mussolini's career before 1919
◆ The formation of the Fascist movement
◆ The revival of Fascism
◆ The road to respectability
◆ The March on Rome

Mussolini's career before 1919

Mussolini's youth and early life

Benito Mussolini was born in 1883 in a village in the north-eastern province of Romagna. His father was a hard-drinking, womanising blacksmith of revolutionary socialist views. His mother was a gentler creature – a devout Catholic who taught in the local school. The young Mussolini inherited his father's socialism and at school he was a violent bully, resentful of conformity and discipline. His talent for public speaking, though, was recognised and at the age of seventeen he gave a speech in the local theatre to commemorate the Italian composer, Giuseppe Verdi.

Somewhat surprisingly, Mussolini qualified as a teacher, but he could only keep order by bribing his pupils with sweets. He had two stints as a schoolmaster, interrupted by a period as a casual labourer in Switzerland as well as two years of military service. In his late teens, again like his father, he became an inveterate womaniser. Throughout his life he liked the company of admiring women, and later boasted that he had never had any male friends.

Mussolini the journalist

In 1908 Mussolini found his vocation as a journalist, editing a socialist journal while still working as a teacher. He then moved to the Austrian-ruled, Italian-speaking town of Trent where he spent a year. Returning to the region of his birth, he became editor of a weekly socialist magazine in the town of Forli. The Italian invasion of Libya in 1911 gave him an opportunity to establish himself as a firebrand: he helped to organise violent anti-war riots and spent five months in prison as a result. He emerged a local socialist hero. In 1912 he became a national figure when he was appointed editor of the socialist daily newspaper *Avanti!*.

His revolutionary views fitted in with the radicals who had taken control of the leadership of the PSI during the Libyan war. His journalistic style anticipated the modern tabloids: he composed dramatic headlines, wrote vitriolic and lurid stories and simplified issues. But he doubled the circulation of the paper.

Mussolini and the First World War

At the start of the war, Mussolini followed the socialist line, condemning it as imperialist. But by October his views had changed and he advocated what he called 'active neutrality' in sympathy with Britain and France. He resigned from *Avanti!* and set up his own newspaper called Il *Popolo d'Italia* (The People of Italy) backed by cash from various sympathisers including northern business-men, the Italian government and possibly some French and British supporters. The first edition appeared on 15 November 1914 and demanded that Italy join the war. Mussolini's decision to become a supporter of intervention, however, relegated him to political obscurity. In September 1915 Mussolini was called up and served two years in the army. A wound ended his military career in 1917, and he returned to journalism. His war experience was important to him, as it enabled him to claim the comradeship of other soldiers when he founded the Fascist movement after the war. His articles in Il *Popolo d'Italia* meanwhile thundered against the politicians and anti-war socialists, striking a chord with the strident nationalism that swept Italy after the defeat at Caporetto.

The formation of the Fascist movement

Mussolini's creation of the *Fascio Italiano di Combattimento* in March 1919 was a typical piece of extravagant self-advertisement. It was not particularly success-ful. No one can be sure exactly how many people attended the inaugural meeting – Mussolini later said that it was only 45 because he wanted to claim that they were a small, dedicated band of revolutionaries. Most historians, however, reckon there were about 100. They later became known as 'Fascists of the First Hour'. After 1922, when it became fashionable and advantageous to have been a founding member, their number increased dramatically.

They were an odd assortment of ex-soldiers, former socialists, National Syndicalists and Futurists. The meeting, in the words of historian Adrian Lyttelton, 'was designed both to preserve the tradition of the first interven-tionist *fasci* and to capture the mood of post-war discontent and undirected revolt. It was to be the vehicle for the protest of the new forces thrown up by the war against the constraint of rules, organisations and bureaucracies.' This explains why the meeting did not adopt a programme or manifesto. Mussolini wanted to create not a party, but a *movement*, which would have the flexibility to attract a wide range of support.

The importance of the arditi

Among the important early recruits to Fascism were former members of Italy's elite units – the black-shirted *arditi*. They did not easily adapt to civilian life once they were demobilised, and remained in touch with each other through ex-servicemen's organisations. Their leader, Ferruccio Vecchi, attended Mussolini's inaugural Fascist meeting. Less than a month later Vecchi led a bunch of *ex-arditi* in a raid that destroyed the Milan office and printing works of

Avanti!. This success encouraged Mussolini to recruit a private army from the *ex-arditi*, and he was soon using the filing cabinets at his editorial office for storing guns and explosives.

Early failure

Mussolini's ideas did not amount to a coherent or credible political pro-gramme. This was partly because Mussolini could not decide exactly what he believed in, but it was also because it gave him the freedom to adopt any point of view that would make a good headline and attract attention and support. When the Fascists fought their first election in November 1919, most local groups drew up their own political programmes. Some were much more right-wing than Mussolini's. This did not bother him. From the start, the *Fasci di Combattimento* boasted that they were a flexible group without a strict party mechanism or rigid programme. Their structure was so loose that members of the movement could belong to other organisations.

However, Mussolini's decision to contest the election of 1919 was unwise. Not a single Fascist was elected and, even in their Milan stronghold, Mussolini and his Fascist colleagues achieved fewer than 5,000 votes out of the 270,000 cast. The new movement – which in August had boasted 70 separate *fasci* throughout the country – appeared to be dead. By the end of the year the Milan Central Committee was admitting that there were only 31 *fasci* in Italy, with a total membership of 870. For a time, Mussolini contemplated emigrating.

The revival of Fascism

Mussolini recovered his self-confidence and stayed in Italy, but initially he was uncertain about the direction Fascism should take. With socialism seemingly in the ascendant, he was sufficiently opportunistic to hold a secret meeting in September with some of the strikers who had occupied their factories, offering to lead an insurrection. He abandoned the idea when the strikes collapsed.

D'Annunzio's seizure of Fiume presented Mussolini with a dilemma. In public, he had to give D'Annunzio's patriotic bravado wholehearted support. But he had no desire to play second fiddle to another nationalist. He was relieved when the regime in Fiume collapsed, even though he lost support among some of the *ex-arditi* for not backing D'Annunzio more enthusiastically.

The drift to the right

During 1920 Mussolini began to sense that, if it was to succeed, Fascism would have to become a right-wing movement. At the first Fascist national congress in May, anti-capitalist rhetoric was replaced by calls for class collaboration. Mussolini then abandoned the anti-Catholic slogans in his programme and looked for support from conservative businessmen. He even allowed his Milan 'black-shirts' to be used as strike-breakers and security guards for industrial firms. The collapse of the factory occupation in September finally convinced him that the workers were not powerful enough to overthrow the state.

Mussolini ordered his regional bosses to organise their 'Black-shirt' squads along paramilitary lines. He was aware that controlling the streets and squares of Italian cities and towns – known as 'piazza politics' – was more important

The strike of 1922 – breaking the strike increased Fascist popularity.

than the socialist tactic of occupying factories and calling strikes. Violence would bring notoriety, attention and support to the Fascist movement. Mussolini also realised that the authorities were reluctant to punish Fascist violence severely, provided that it was directed against the left. The feebleness of the socialists' response demonstrated that they had neither the inclination nor the organisation to resist in kind.

Rural 'vigilante' Fascism

Ironically, though, the revival of Fascism owed little to Mussolini. Rural Fascism, for example, developed spontaneously in the Po Valley towards the end of 1920, and its local leaders looked to Mussolini for inspiration and support rather than direction.

It began in Ferrara and Bologna. On 15 September 1920, with the local elections approaching, nine men in the town of Ferrara met to revive their local *fascio*. Within two months they had enrolled nearly a thousand members. In contrast to the previous year, the local bourgeoisie was eager to support them. Both landowners and the middle classes in the region had become fed up with the gains that the socialists had made during the *biennio rosso*, and had lost faith in the power of the authorities to do anything about it. They were reassured by the moves to the right that Fascism had made during 1920 and, with their incomes falling as the Italian economy moved into recession, landowners were determined to resist further demands from the socialists.

The *fascio* immediately organised a 'special vigilante squad' to protect strike-breaking blackleg labour. On election day socialists were beaten up at polling stations. In November in nearby Bologna Fascists opened fire on socialists as they arrived to be installed in the newly elected administration. On 20 December four Fascists and a Socialist were killed in a clash in the town square of Ferrara. The incident was unfairly blamed exclusively on the socialists, and caused a wave of indignation. Furthermore it stimulated Fascist recruitment and encouraged the authorities to crack down on the left.

By the spring of 1921, events in Ferrara and Bologna had transformed the nature of Fascism from an urban phenomenon into a rural one. At the end of March, the *fascio* in Rome had 1,480 members and Turin a mere 581. Ferrara, on the other hand, had nearly 7,000 members, and Bologna more than 5,000. This rural success was soon duplicated in the rest of the Po Valley and spread south to Tuscany and Umbria. Between March and May national membership figures mushroomed from 80,000 to 187,000.

The Fascist ras

The rapid growth of rural Fascism owed a great deal to the energy, ruthlessness and organisational ability of local leaders (known as *ras* in imitation of Abyssinian chieftains) who exploited the loose framework of the movement and built independent baronies for themselves. Italo Balbo established himself as boss in Ferrara, Roberto Farinacci in Cremona, Dino Grandi in Bologna and Augusto Turati in Brescia. They ran systematic campaigns of intimidation and violence to destroy socialism in their regions and establish their own control. Apart from attacking leaders and smashing up premises, they organised tax strikes to make it impossible for socialist councils to govern, and forced the *braccianti* to leave socialist unions and join fascist ones which renegotiated labour contracts in favour of the employers.

Why was rural Fascism so successful?

The Fascist counter-revolution was particularly successful in the Po Valley because it received the enthusiastic support of two distinct social groups. The large landowners who employed the *braccianti* were prepared to finance and equip the squads. But Fascism was also supported by the lower middle class: shopkeepers who disliked socialist price controls, and share-croppers and small peasant proprietors who were frightened by the socialist aim of collectivising the land. The Fascist advance was slower in areas such as Tuscany and Apulia, where it was more obvious that the squads were merely doing the dirty work of the landowners. In the words of historian Philip Morgan: 'Generally outside Ferrara, agrarian Fascism finally broke the back of socialist rural organisations during the winter to spring of 1921–22, often with the help of battle-hardened squads from neighbouring provinces.' Fascism made no impact in the remote areas, particularly in the south, where socialism was weak. Rural Fascism was exclusively a reaction to the strength of socialism.

The road to respectability

Mussolini had never expected rural Fascism to be successful, and he was both pleased and appalled by its rapid growth. On the one hand, he welcomed the increased size and significance that rural Fascism gave to the movement – by the end of 1921 Fascist membership had increased to 250,000. However, he was also worried that Fascism might slip out of his control, especially as the *ras* had no taste for electoral politics and Mussolini wanted to see if he could acquire power by legal means.

The general election of May 1921

In May 1921, prime minister Giolitti called a general election, thinking that socialism was on the wane. In an echo of his pre-war *trasformismo* politics, he tried to bring Fascism into the mainstream by allowing Fascists to join the electoral lists with government candidates (under proportional representation each constituency elected a number of deputies). It was a disastrous mistake. The election was marred by an orgy of Fascist violence, with 40 people killed on polling day alone. The *ras* of the Po Valley were especially active, and their intimidation of potential socialist voters was extremely successful. The violence was ignored by local state authorities, who convinced themselves that it was legitimate because Fascist candidates were backed by the government. Even so, only 35 Fascists were elected, Mussolini among them. The vote for the PSI held up well despite the violence, and they remained the largest party in the new parliament. Giolitti resigned with his final attempt at *trasformismo* in tatters.

The Pact of Pacification, August 1921

In his first few speeches in parliament Mussolini appeared to confirm that Fascism had become a right-wing movement seeking to preserve the establishment against the radical left. But in August he suddenly made an astonishing reversal by offering a pact of reconciliation to the PSI – an action that has become a matter of debate among historians. Some attribute it to Mussolini's opportunism, arguing that he was so desperate for power that he would ally with anyone to get it. Others see it as a bid to tame the *ras*. They argue that Mussolini was worried that the scale and ferocity of Fascist violence were getting out of control and might provoke the government to use the army to suppress the movement. This meant he needed to assert his control and demonstrate that extreme violence was no longer necessary.

The *ras* were furious. Their power was based on violence and they were not convinced that the socialist enemy was defeated. Many of them were syndicalists who despised parliament and dreamed of a genuine social revolution that would unite Italians in a national community of employers and workers, landowners and peasants. Balbo and Grandi led the opposition to the pact. They organised a congress in Bologna to trumpet their opposition, and even sounded out D'Annunzio as a possible replacement for Mussolini.

The formation of the Fascist Party, November 1921

Mussolini and the *ras* soon realised that they needed each other. Mussolini knew that he could not alienate his rank-and-file, and the regional bosses were aware that their authority would soon disappear if the Fascists did not come to power nationally. Only Mussolini was well enough known to be a national leader. This is what Balbo meant when he remarked: 'it is impossible to halt our actions at this point. Fascism is not a static party. The local situations do not count if the life of the whole nation does not change ... We must conquer the nation.' So in November 1921 a compromise was reached. Mussolini abandoned the pact of pacification and the *ras* agreed to the formation of the *Partito Nazionale Fascista* (PNF – National Fascist Party). The establishment of the PNF gave Mussolini a degree of central control, but the *ras* ensured that they remained in control of their squads.

The March on Rome

In February 1922 another short-lived coalition government collapsed. There was little chance of building an effective replacement: the liberal deputies were divided into four different factions, grouped around former prime ministers, and the two major parties were also badly divided.

The PPI with 107 seats, could not agree on their attitude to Fascism. Their leader, Sturzo, disliked the Fascists and was supported by many local party activists who were being attacked by Fascist thugs for their role in helping the peasants in the *biennio rosso*. However, a right-wing faction in the PPI admired the Fascists for their anti-socialism and wanted an accommodation with them. In February 1922, Sturzo was compromised by the election to the Papacy of Pius XI, a former archbishop of Milan who had blessed Fascist banners. Pius used his authority as Pope to obstruct any attempt by Sturzo to co-operate in an anti-Fascist coalition.

The PSI had been weakened in January 1921 when some of their members broke away to form the Communist Party. In the election of 1921 the Communists won fifteen seats – not enough to make them powerful, but enough to add credibility to Fascist propaganda about the red threat. The PSI, with 123 deputies, was still the largest in parliament, but its leaders underestimated the Fascist threat, continuing to believe that the crisis of capitalism, which would usher in their rule, was not far away. They vetoed any attempt by more moderate Socialists to join an anti-Fascist coalition. Some of the moderates were even expelled from the Party for being willing to collaborate with a bourgeois government and formed a new party called the Socialist Unity Party (PSU).

Fascist advances

During the spring and summer of 1922 the Fascist assault on power in the localities continued. The *ras* wanted to present Mussolini with a *fait accompli* and start an armed assault on power to overthrow the parliamentary establishment they despised so much. On 11 May Italo Balbo took possession of Ferrara with more than 40,000 Black-shirts and agricultural workers. He claimed that he wanted the prefect to order a programme of public works that would reduce unemployment, and he ostentatiously withdrew when the order was given. His real reason for the occupation, as he privately admitted, was as a 'thermometer of our strength'. When the prefect of neighbouring Bologna asked the government for troops to prevent the same thing happening to him, the Fascists promptly entered the town to force his removal. In July Roberto Farinacci launched his Fascist squads against the Socialist council in Cremona.

These developments presented Mussolini with an opportunity and two problems. The Fascist assault on power strengthened his hand in bargaining with parliamentary leaders – he could demand to be included in the government as the only man capable of restoring law and order. On the other hand, Fascist violence might get out of control and provoke the government to use the army against the Black-shirts. This briefly looked as if it was a possibility when events in Cremona caused a parliamentary vote of no confidence in the prime minister. Fortunately for Mussolini, the paralysis in parliament prevented the formation of a government that might have taken a tougher line with Fascist illegality. Mussolini's second problem was that Fascist violence might expose the contradictions simmering beneath the surface of the movement.

Explaining Fascist success 1919–1922

The appeal of Fascism

Many Italians regarded the existing system as weak and corrupt
- Fascism promised strong government

Fascist violence
- was directed against the left
- showed that Fascism was strong and ruthless

Nationalism had a wide appeal
- Fascism promised to make Italy strong

Fascist ideology was vague, promising something for everyone
- it seemed to offer an end to class divisions
- some liked its anti-socialism
- some liked its revolutionary syndicalism

Fascism seemed new and exciting
- young people were attracted by the emphasis on action and change
- discontented groups hoped that Fascism would smash the old system

Fascist propaganda was impressive
uniforms, parades and marches suggested that Fascism was dynamic

The weaknesses of liberal Italy

Governments seemed weak and corrupt
- elections were 'managed' especially in the south
- all governments were short-lived coalitions

Post-war conditions further undermined democracy
- high inflation
- unemployment
- industrial unrest

Influential elite groups such as industrialists and landowners were pleased by the anti-socialist violence of the Fascists against
- factory workers
- peasants

Italy's political parties were weak and divided
- PPI: Pope Pius XI against Luigi Sturzo
- liberals: bickering factions
- left-wing: divided into three

Trade unions divided in the same way as the left-wing parties
- moderate socialists
- radical socialist
- communists

The 'Roman Question' remained unanswered
- Pope's ban on political activity was only lifted in 1918
- The Vatican had disagreements with the PPI

The mistakes of Fascism's opponents

Governments responded weakly when challenged
- D'Annunzio's seizure of Fiume
- The chaos of the *biennio rosso*
- The 'March on Rome'

Liberal politicians believed that Fascism could be tamed and controlled
- Giolitti and the election of 1921
- Mussolini's coalition partners in October 1922

Influential individuals failed to oppose Fascism
- the King
- the Pope

The left played into Mussolini's hands
- The general strike of August 1922

Mussolini's skill and opportunism

He owned *Il Popolo d'Italia*
- an important propaganda tool

Timely concessions to the establishment
- abandonment of socialist aims in 1920
- decision to enter parliament in 1921
- willingness to form a coalition government

Keeping the Fascist extremists happy
- abandonment of the pact of pacification in 1921
- support for fascist violence

Using the threat of squad violence to pressure the elites
- the 'March on Rome'

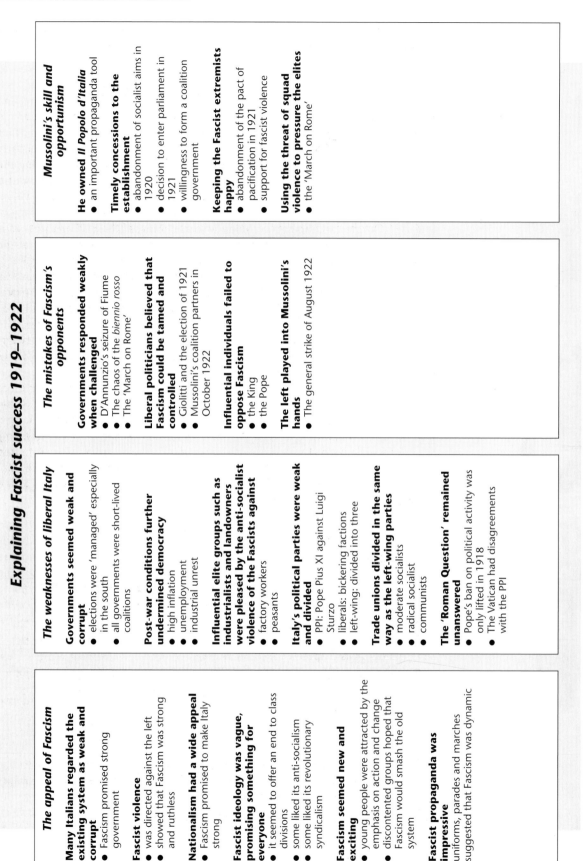

On 12 September 1922 there was a gun battle between rival Fascists in Ferrara over whether they should support landowners or peasants.

The appointment of Mussolini as prime minister

At the end of July 1922, Mussolini's opponents handed him another gift. A strike was called by the Alliance of Labour (a loose association of trade unions trying to resist wage cuts). The strike lasted only four days and was not well supported, but it gave the Fascists an excuse to mobilise their squads on a massive scale and assault the towns and cities where socialism was still strong. Fascist volunteers took the opportunity to run the public services and pose for the benefit of the middle classes as the party of law and order.

On 16 October, Mussolini met the senior members of the PNF and the *ras* to plan the Fascist 'March on Rome'. Given that the Fascists were, in effect, running much of Italy, as town after town came under the control of the squads, he could scarcely do otherwise without destroying his movement. He was still hoping that the politicians would hand him power, making the march unnecessary. A massive rally of 40,000 Fascists at Naples on 24 October kept up the pressure. Mussolini's speech cleverly kept his options open. 'Legality or illegality?' he asked. 'Victory by means of parliament, or through insurrection? Through what paths will Fascism become the State?' He demanded key posts in the cabinet and threatened to march if they were not granted.

During the night of 27–28 October, Fascists began occupying government buildings in provincial capitals all over Italy, preparatory to a march on Rome the next day. The government prepared to resist and drew up a decree for the king to sign, proclaiming martial law. Having initially agreed to sign it, the king then refused – he did not want to be responsible for starting what he feared might be a civil war. On 29 October he asked Mussolini (who was still in Milan) to form a government. Mussolini travelled by train from Milan to Rome, where he was sworn in as prime minister on 30 October.

Studying the growth of the Fascist movement

1   Some historians regard Mussolini as nothing more than an opportunist. Others see him as a politician of considerable skill. What evidence can you find in this chapter for each of these views?

2   Should Fascism be seen as left-wing or right-wing? Make two columns on a piece of paper. In one column, list the left-wing aspects of Fascism and, in the other column, its right-wing features.

3   Why do you think the socialists were unable to resist rural Fascism more effectively?

4   The Fascists might not have come to power if resistance to them had been stronger. What decisions, taken by Mussolini's opponents, served to help him? How important were they?

5   Could Fascism have succeeded without being violent?

The steps to dictatorship, 1922–26

Consolidation

Key Points

- ◆ Mussolini's position in 1922
- ◆ Appeasing the radicals
- ◆ Winning over the conservative establishment
- ◆ The Acerbo Electoral Law
- ◆ The Matteotti Crisis
- ◆ Dictatorship established

Mussolini's position in 1922

When Mussolini was appointed Prime Minister on 30 October 1922 his aim was to remain in power for a long time, but he had no fixed ideas about how to achieve it. Many Italians thought that his government was unlikely to last much longer than those of his predecessors. There was only a handful of Fascist MPs in the Chamber of Deputies and the new government, like so many before it, was a coalition.

Mussolini had achieved power by being deliberately vague about his aims (possibly because he did not know what they were) and this had enabled him to convince different groups that Fascism would solve their problems. The conservative figures of the establishment – the King, the military leaders, the

Mussolini had considerable support from many sections of the Italian population.

industrialists and landowners, and even many deputies in parliament – regarded him as a strong man who would safeguard their interests against the left. But there were many in the Fascist Party, including the Syndicalists and most of the *ras* and their squads, who wanted Mussolini to sweep away the old system and start a truly Fascist revolution.

Over the next few years, Mussolini showed himself to be a master of opportunistic tactics as he manoeuvred between the various individuals and factions seeking his support. He was assisted by the short-sighted squabbling among his potential opponents and a good deal of luck. The in-fighting enabled him, as he said at the time, to pluck his opponents 'like a chicken, one feather at a time'. By 1925 his domination of Italian politics was firmly established.

The formation of Mussolini's government

When he arrived in Rome for his audience with the King on 30 October, Mussolini is said to have remarked, 'Your Majesty, I have come from the battle-field, fortunately bloodless.' But he was shrewd enough to realise that he needed to mix this emphasis on the power of the *squadristi* with subtle appeasement of the establishment. To reinforce the myth of a Fascist seizure of power, he allowed the squads to parade past the royal palace on 31 October, but when he formed his cabinet of thirteen ministers, it contained only four Fascists. He appointed a General and an Admiral to the two service ministries, thereby reassuring the armed forces that there was no immediate threat of the Fascist squads usurping their role. He even thought about appointing a moderate socialist from the PSU to emphasise the national appeal of his new government, but was persuaded, possibly by some Milanese industrialists, to change his mind.

Mussolini emphasised the Fascist character of his government by taking three Cabinet posts himself. As well as prime minister, he made himself Foreign Minister and Minister of the Interior. Mussolini ensured that the enforcement of law and order was firmly in Fascist hands by making Michele Bianchi, the secretary of the Fascist Party, his Deputy at the Ministry of the Interior and appointing General De Bono (one of the earliest recruits to Fascism) Chief of Police. He also allocated offices in the Ministry of the Interior to some of his more disreputable followers. These included Amerigo Dumini, a criminal thug who led a secret gang of hit men (called the *Cheka* in imitation of Lenin's secret police in the USSR), which terrorised political opponents.

Mussolini in Parliament

Mussolini was still ambiguous about his aims when he first faced the Chamber of Deputies as prime minister on 16 November. He intimidated his audience by announcing that, with the Fascist squads behind him, he could have closed down parliament, but that he preferred to rule with their co-operation. The Chamber of Deputies and the Senate each responded with a huge vote of confidence, granting his government emergency powers for twelve months. Most parliamentarians deceived themselves into believing that Mussolini was acting constitutionally by seeking parliamentary consent for his government, and that his tough measures would be directed against the left. Only the PSI voted against him in parliament and even some of those were pleased to see a strong ruler destroying the political institutions of Italy's liberal, bourgeois democracy.

The violence of the Fascist squadristi

There followed a wave of violence, especially in the big cities, as local Fascist gangs set out to destroy their opponents and establish themselves in power. Three opposition deputies were killed and fifty more were attacked, usually in broad daylight and in public. A favourite punishment was to force victims to drink castor oil, sometimes mixed with petrol, which often proved fatal. The terror even spread abroad, because the Fascists were particularly savage with any former members of the Party who, having fled, revealed the extent of corruption and violence within the movement. Mussolini was delighted with this reign of terror and even told Dumini which victims to attack. He knew that, as long as the violence was directed against the left, he would face little criticism from his coalition partners and conservative supporters.

Mussolini's dilemma

The violence of the squads also reminded Mussolini that there were many in the Fascist movement who were impatient with the pace of change and who looked forward to a complete Fascist take-over of Italy. Syndicalists within the Fascist Party expected the formation of Mussolini's government to be immediately followed by the creation of syndicates in industry and agriculture. These would control employers as well as workers and peasants to ensure that the economy was run in the national interest. The Syndicalists' demand for rapid and fundamental change was supported by the *ras*, who wanted to entrench their positions of local power by replacing the machinery of state government with the Fascist Party and the squads.

Mussolini was wary of these demands. He knew that his conservative supporters were happy to see both socialism and liberal democracy destroyed, but he also knew that they did not want the country to be run by Fascist thugs. Nor did Mussolini want to de-centralise power and allow the *ras* to run their regions as private empires – he wanted a centralised dictatorship with power in his own hands. However, he was also aware that he needed the squads, both to destroy his political opponents and to keep himself in power. Without the squads – which he claimed numbered 300,000 – his government would be no different from any of its predecessors. He realised that he needed to demonstrate to his supporters that a new Fascist state would be created as well as finding a means of bringing the Party's radicals under control.

Appeasing the radicals

The Fascist Party

Because he had complete control of the Ministry of the Interior, Mussolini was able to ensure that Fascist violence went unpunished. He announced an official amnesty for Fascists accused of political violence, and even ordered that any Fascists who had been killed in the fighting should be treated as war heroes and awarded state pensions.

In December 1922 Mussolini established the Fascist Grand Council – an alternative Cabinet consisting entirely of nominees from the Fascist Party. Although it had no legal status until 1928, the Fascist Grand Council increasingly usurped the functions of the Cabinet, especially once the institutions of democracy had been destroyed.

The squadristi

Mussolini's solution to the problem posed by the squads was to transform them, in January 1923, into the Fascist Militia (*Milizia volontaria per la sicurezza nazionale*: MVSN) answerable to himself, commanded by General De Bono, and paid for by the state. He hoped that this would enable him to control the rank-and-file squad members and undermine the independent power of the *ras*. At the same time it gave him a private army whose function was to guard buildings, organise parades and act as a visible sign of Fascist power. The creation of the MVSN was not, however, a total solution. The *ras* continued to make trouble for Mussolini for several more years and the army disliked the Militia as a potential rival.

Winning over the conservative establishment

● **The merger with the Nationalists**
When he formed his first Cabinet in October 1922, Mussolini appointed the Nationalist leader, Luigi Federzone, to the post of Colonial Minister. The Nationalists were a small party with only ten deputies, but they enjoyed close links with influential figures in business and the armed forces. They also ran a private militia of 80,000 Blue-shirts who had frequently clashed with the Fascist Black-shirts before Mussolini's appointment. In February 1923 they decided to merge with the Fascist Party – an important development because the influence of the Nationalists helped the Fascists to win the 1924 election in the south where Fascism was weakest. The addition of the Blueshirts to the MVSN also provided Mussolini with a useful counterweight to the power of the *ras*.

● **The** *Confindustria* **and the** *Agrari*
The *Confederazione dell'Industria Italiana* – the *Confindustria* – was a national association of major industrial leaders. Its members welcomed the appointment of Mussolini because they wanted to see a strong man in power who would crush the left, but they were worried about the ambitions of the syndicalist Fascists. Mussolini eased their fears by allowing them to organise their own syndicates, separate from those of the workers. His economic policies were designed to gain their support: taxes were lowered, price and rent controls were abolished, the telephone system and state life insurance schemes were privatised and government regulation of corporate finance was reduced. Mussolini continued this conciliatory policy towards the landed class. The law on land reform was suspended, death duties were reduced by half and government subsidies to agricultural co-operatives were withdrawn.

● **The PPI and the Pope**
The PPI had been divided over their attitude to Fascism before Mussolini's appointment, and he widened the split by including two right-wing members of their party in his coalition. The majority of the PPI, under the influence of their leader Luigi Sturzo, became opponents of the government.

Pope Pius XI, who had never liked Sturzo's hostility to Fascism, decided that direct negotiations with Mussolini would be a much better way of settling the 'Roman Question' and securing the interests of the Church than relying on the PPI. In January 1923 the Pope's secretary of state held a secret meeting with Mussolini at which they discussed the long-standing problem of the Church's relations with the Italian state, and Mussolini is thought to have offered government assistance for the Catholic *Banca di Roma*. Mussolini then seduced the Vatican with more concessions. He promised to make religious instruction compulsory in schools, declared Freemasonry incompatible with Fascism, offered support for a new Catholic university in Milan, and banned the distribution of contraceptives.

When the Party Congress of the PPI met in Turin in April 1923 and offered only conditional support for the Fascist government, Mussolini dismissed the two PPI members of his government. The Pope then effectively completed the job of routing the PPI by engineering the resignation of Sturzo from the party leadership in July 1923 and banishing him from Italy a year later.

The Acerbo Electoral Law

Despite the weakness of the PPI, the dismissal of their two ministers from the government undermined Mussolini's already weak position in the Chamber of Deputies. To ensure that the government gained an outright majority in the next parliament, the Fascist deputy Giacomo Acerbo introduced a bill to reform the electoral system. Under his proposal, the party or coalition winning the largest number of votes (provided it received more than 25 per cent of the votes cast) would be allocated two-thirds of the seats in the new Chamber.

Reactions to the Electoral Law

Only the Socialists and Communists voted against the Acerbo Bill. It was a measure of the confusion and weakness of the PPI that, despite the reservations of most Catholic deputies about Mussolini, their official policy was to abstain. That did not stop 39 deputies resigning from the party in order to support the Bill. Many of the liberal factions voted in favour because they believed Mussolini's propaganda about the need for a strong government. Doubtless the presence of armed Black-shirts in the Chamber, ostentatiously paring their nails with their daggers while the deputies voted, helped to convince many waverers. In the Chamber of Deputies the bill was carried by 303 votes to 140. In the Senate it received an even bigger endorsement of 165 votes to 41.

The election campaign was accompanied by a further wave of terror, and the results, which gave the Fascists and their allies 66 per cent of the votes and 374 deputies, appeared to suggest that the Acerbo Law had been unnecessary. In the Fascist heartlands of Ferrara, Tuscany and Emilia, Fascist candidates swept the board, but in the south, where support for Fascism was weak, the old, corrupt electoral politics still delivered the votes. Nationalists, conservative Catholics and even some liberals were elected as coalition partners of the Fascists because they exercised local power and patronage. Historian Philip Morgan estimates that only 60 per cent of the deputies in the new Chamber were Fascists. The rest he describes as 'fellow travellers' who were 'now adopting the Fascist label'.

The Matteotti Crisis

On 30 May 1924 the leader of the Socialist Unity Party (PSU), Giacomo Matteotti, a well-known critic of Mussolini, made a speech in the Chamber of Deputies denouncing the violence and intimidation that had accompanied the election campaign. He claimed that Mussolini had no right to govern because his power was based on a fraudulent election result. Mussolini was furious at Matteotti's defiance. So, too, was Cesari Rossi, the head of his press office, who was a leading figure in the 'moderate' faction of the Fascist Party. The moderates hoped that the decisive election result would enable Mussolini to base his regime on a programme of laws passed by the Chamber and marginalise the extremist *ras* who wanted to destroy the old system.

The murder of Matteotti

On 10 June 1924 Matteotti disappeared. Eye-witnesses came forward who had seen him being bundled into a car. When police enquiries traced the car, its blood-stained interior suggested that Matteotti had been murdered, although his body was not discovered until 16 August. The car was owned by a friend of Cesari Rossi and the police established that the assassins were Amerigo Dumini and other members of the *Cheka* who were in the pay of Giovanni Marinelli and Aldo Finzi – senior officials in the PNF and the Ministry of the Interior respectively. This implicated Mussolini himself in the murder.

When questioned about it in the Chamber of Deputies on 12 June, Mussolini answered evasively. One opposition deputy rounded on him and declared, 'Then he is an accomplice.' Mussolini lost his nerve for several days and could not decide what to do. He acted only when key members of his Cabinet threatened to resign unless he sacrificed some of his henchmen. Finzi was sacked, Rossi and Marinelli were arrested, General De Bono resigned as Chief of Police and Head of the MVSN, and Mussolini handed the Ministry of the Interior over to the Nationalist leader, Luigi Federzone. Amerigo Dumini was imprisoned for his part in the murder. According to historian Denis Mack Smith, Dumini was later paid such vast sums in hush money that his income was greater than that of a Cabinet minister.

Giacomo Matteotti, the PSU leader murdered by the Fascists in June 1924.

The Aventine Secession

With Mussolini apparently vulnerable, the opposition parties decided in late June to withdraw from the Chamber of Deputies. They hoped that this would emphasise Matteotti's claim that the Chamber had been corruptly elected and force the King to dismiss Mussolini. Their withdrawal became known as the Aventine Secession because they were consciously imitating the citizens of ancient Rome who had withdrawn from the city to the Aventine Hill in a successful bid to oppose unjust rule. The move backfired badly. It destroyed any chance that the Chamber of Deputies might vote to remove Mussolini, and provided the King with an excuse to do nothing because, in the absence of a parliamentary vote against Mussolini, he saw no reason to dismiss him.

Reactions to the Matteotti murder

● The King, the Senate and the Pope

The King was unwilling to dismiss Mussolini for the same reason he had appointed him prime minister in the first place: he feared the alternative – a socialist government or civil war. His reluctance to act seemed justified by the Senate on 26 June 1924. Unlike the Chamber, the Senate was not packed with Mussolini's supporters, but it nevertheless gave the government a massive vote of confidence by 225 votes to 21. Their attitude was summed up by the scholar and senator Benedetto Croce who said that Fascism had 'done much good' and 'we must give Fascism time to complete its process of transformation'.

In July the Pope intervened to end discussions between the leaders of the Aventine Secession and the PPI about forming an anti-Fascist coalition. He still regarded socialism as a much more serious threat than Fascism.

● The liberals and the *Confindustria*

Mussolini survived the worst of the crisis because his potential opponents believed that they could extract some political advantage from keeping him in power. Although they voiced some noisy criticism, the leading members of the *Confindustria* and the liberals grouped around the former premiers hoped that the crisis would chasten Mussolini and oblige him to curb the violent excesses of his followers. Like the Pope, they hoped to see Fascism tamed and feared that the alternative would be socialism.

● The army and the militia

The army used the crisis to squeeze concessions from Mussolini. The army's leaders had always been suspicious of the MVSN and feared its pretensions. In June 1924 Mussolini mobilised six legions of the Militia in case his government was challenged on the streets. On that occasion the army provided the Militia with weapons because they did not want to see the triumph of socialism any more than Mussolini did, but the crisis was too good an opportunity for army leaders to miss. In August, they pushed Mussolini into agreeing that the Militia's officers would be ex-army regulars and that its oath of loyalty would be to the King, not just Mussolini.

● The Fascist *ras*

The Matteotti crisis also agitated the *ras*. To them it demonstrated the folly of basing the power of Fascism on the authority of parliament. Mussolini tried to exploit their anger by making a rousing speech to the national council of the

Fascist Party in August. He promised to destroy liberty and supported their demand for a complete Fascist revolution in Italy.

But Mussolini then enraged the *ras* once again by his concessions to the army, which threatened to undermine their control of their squads. They were even more alarmed when Italo Balbo, who had replaced General De Bono as Commander-in-Chief of the Militia, was forced to resign because a court case revealed the violent attacks he had ordered against socialists and his involvement in the murder of the Catholic priest, Don Minzoni. This seemed to the *ras* to be a betrayal of everything that Fascism stood for: to them, Balbo should be praised rather than sacked for attacking the enemies of Fascism. By December 1924 there were rumours of a coup, with the *ras* looking to Balbo for leadership.

The peak of the crisis: December 1924

The crisis reached its height on 27 December when the liberal newspaper *Il Mondo* published a memorandum by Cesare Rossi blaming Mussolini for some of the worst Fascist crimes of the previous two years. Four days later Mussolini faced a delegation of 33 senior Militia commanders who demanded that he immediately clamp down on the opposition and release Fascists from prison. Some accounts of the meeting even suggest that they threatened to replace him if he did not act. Mussolini knew that he had little choice. The Rossi memorandum had destroyed any chance of his remaining as a constitutional prime minister, so the threats of the Militia commanders probably only confirmed him in the action he had already decided to take.

Mussolini promises dictatorship

On 3 January 1925 Mussolini boldly told the Chamber of Deputies that he took full responsibility for Fascism. 'I declare ... that I, and I alone, assume the political, moral and historical responsibility for all that has happened ... If Fascism has been a criminal association, if all the acts of violence have been the result of a certain historical, political and moral climate, the responsibility is mine.' He did not specifically accept responsibility for Matteotti's murder but blamed the opposition for the breakdown of constitutional rule and promised the imposition of tough measures.

With the Aventine parties still boycotting parliament and the King still unwilling to dismiss Mussolini, the remaining deputies were cowed into silence. The speech was immediately followed by the imposition of repressive measures. Opposition meeting-places were closed down and there were widespread arbitrary arrests. Over the next few months further repression followed as Mussolini's dictatorship became firmly established.

Il Duce: *the dictatorship is established*

The legal framework

The formation of Mussolini's dictatorship was largely the work of two former Nationalists, Luigi Federzone at the Ministry of the Interior and Alfredo Rocco, who became Minister of Justice in January 1925. Four unsuccessful attempts to assassinate Mussolini between November 1925 and October 1926 provided them with excellent excuses for their tough measures. These included:

◆ tightening press censorship;

◆ making Mussolini accountable only to the King, not to parliament;

◆ banning secret societies, including the Freemasons;

◆ purging government officials in the civil service;

◆ replacing elected mayors with appointed officials;

◆ appointing a new chief of police and extending his powers;

◆ creating a secret police force – OVRA;

◆ legalising arbitrary arrest;

◆ increasing the government's powers to monitor opposition groups;

◆ banning other political parties;

◆ extending the number of crimes punishable by the death penalty.

Parliament

The Aventine Secession was used to eliminate most of the parliamentary opposition. The government simply declared that those who had withdrawn had forfeited their right to be deputies by leaving the Chamber. In October 1925 the first attempt to assassinate Mussolini provided an opportunity to ban Matteotti's socialist party, the PSU. The fourth attempt in October 1926 was followed by a ban on all opposition parties.

The emasculation of parliament was complete by 1928. Under a new electoral law introduced in May, voters were presented with a list of approved candidates to be accepted or rejected *en bloc*. Only the Senate, whose members were appointed by the monarch, retained some independence. In December 1928 the Fascist Grand Council was given legal status as 'the supreme organ which co-ordinates and controls all the activities of the regime'. Since Mussolini decided when the Fascist Grand Council would meet and what it would discuss, this merely underlined his ascendancy.

The Fascist Party

Although Mussolini had, to some extent, been pushed into dictatorship by his Fascist *ras* in December 1924, he was determined not to be controlled by them, nor to allow the Fascist Party to take over the running of the state. His solution was a bold one. He selected the most violent and outspoken of the *ras*, Roberto Farinacci, and made him national secretary of the PNF in February 1925. Farinacci launched the Fascist squads in a new wave of terror against their regime's remaining opponents, but he also purged the membership of the PNF and centralised its organisation. Mussolini decided that the violence had gone far enough when, in October 1925, foreign tourists witnessed the killing of some Freemasons and liberals in Florence. He ordered the squads to be dissolved and, in March 1926, dismissed Farinacci. The new party secretary was Augusto Turati, former *ras* of Brescia. Turati carried out more purges of the party member-ship and, in October 1926, replaced the local election of party officials with

Five reasons for the successful establishment of Mussolini's dictatorship

---

Reason 1   Mussolini seduced different conservative groups

The Confindustria and the landowners *supported Mussolini because*
- the Fascist squads were destroying socialism
- Mussolini's economic policies suited them
- he allowed them to water down Fascist syndicalism

The Catholic Church *supported Mussolini because*
- the Fascist squads were destroying socialism
- Mussolini offered financial help
- he introduced policies specifically to gain Church support

The King *supported Mussolini because*
- Mussolini promised to end Italy's political instability
- the King feared civil war if Fascism was denied power
- Mussolini seemed willing to respect the monarchy and the army

The Army *supported Mussolini because*
- the Fascist squads were destroying socialism
- the Army was unwilling to suppress Fascism by force
- Mussolini subordinated the Militia to the Army

Reason 2   Potential opposition groups were badly divided

The left *was divided into three parties*
- the Communist Party (PCI) split from the Socialists in January 1921
- the moderate Socialists formed their own party (PSU) in October 1922
- the main Socialist Party (PSI) refused to join a 'bourgeois' coalition against Fascism

The Roman Catholic Popular Party (PPI) *was divided over its attitude towards Fascism*
- right-wing members of the Party preferred Fascism to socialism
- left-wing members sympathised with workers and peasants against Fascism

The Liberals *were ineffective*
- there were at least four liberal 'factions' grouped around former prime ministers
- most liberals preferred Mussolini to his more radical followers and hoped that, if they co-operated with him, he would bring Fascist extremism under control

---

Reason 3   Fascism was extremely popular with Italy's middle classes

- there was little popular enthusiasm for the institutions of democracy that Fascism destroyed
- Fascism offered protection from socialism and communism
- Mussolini appeared to be a strong leader, able to end Italy's instability and weakness
- only Fascism seemed capable of making Italy strong abroad

Reason 4   Fascist violence intimidated and disorientated political opponents

- leading opponents of Fascism were threatened, beaten up or killed
- opposition meetings, offices and newspapers were regularly attacked and destroyed
- even moderate, co-operative politicians were intimidated by Fascist displays of force

---

Reason 5   Mussolini displayed considerable opportunist political skills

- he made timely gestures to the establishment to make them think he would control Fascist extremism
- he made gestures to the *ras* and the Fascist syndicalists to keep them loyal
- in December 1924, once he was sure he would not be dismissed by the King, he accepted the *ras'* demand that he establish a dictatorship

appointment from above. This neutered the PNF: by the 1930s, it had become, in the words of historian Martin Blinkhorn, 'an inflated bureaucracy of time-serving careerists, largely devoid of a creative political role'.

Studying the steps to dictatorship

1 The establishment of Mussolini's dictatorship was made easier for him by the mistakes of his potential opponents. Identify the misjudgements made by each of the following individuals and groups:-
the King
the opposition parties in the Chamber of Deputies
the Pope
Italy's landowners and industrialists
the army leaders

2 The Fascist *ras* and the *squadristi* were both a hindrance and a help to Mussolini.
a) Identify the problems they posed him.
b) To what extent was his power based on the violence of the *squadristi*? How did the *ras* help him to retain and extend his power?

3 Identify as many examples as you can of Mussolini's political skill during the period between his appointment as prime minister in October 1922 and the resolution of the Matteotti crisis in January 1925.

Issues and Interpretations

Did Italian Fascism ever really exist?

The nature of Italian Fascism

Mussolini was one of the first to describe Italy as 'totalitarian' when he declared in 1932 that 'for the Fascist, everything is in the State, and nothing human or spiritual exists, much less has value, outside the State. In this sense Fascism is totalitarian.' But the reality was rather different. Mussolini never achieved in Italy the total ascendancy attained by Hitler in Germany or Stalin in the USSR. Too many compromises had been made with powerful interest-groups during his rise to power. The king remained head of state throughout the Fascist era, and even played a part in Mussolini's overthrow in 1943. The army, the Church and the industrialists all retained a degree of autonomy, supporting the regime because it suited them to do so and because Mussolini was generally prepared to leave them alone. Italian Fascism also lacked the ideological consistency of the obsessively racist Nazis.

Many historians and commentators have thus questioned whether Italian Fascism ever amounted to anything. As early as 1923 a Fascist intellectual claimed that the movement lacked 'an organic and clearly defined central idea'. Historian AJP Taylor was scathingly dismissive of Italian Fascism. 'Fascism was ... revolution by fraud: talk without action. There was no new policy, no social transformation, only dictatorship for its own sake. Mussolini lived for show. He did little ... Fascism provided only display: marches, rhetoric, fancy dress' (*From Sarajevo to Potsdam*, 1966). Mussolini's English biographer, Denis Mack Smith (*Mussolini*, 1981), is inclined to agree. He believes that Mussolini was an opportunist whose Fascism movement was nothing more than a vehicle for power. In 1979 an American historian claimed that attempting to define Fascism was like looking for a black cat in a dark, and probably empty, room.

A European phenomenon

And yet Fascism was the dominant issue of European politics between the wars, especially in the 1930s. Dictatorships were much more common than democracies in Europe. Italy, Germany, Spain, Portugal and many of the countries of central and eastern Europe were ruled at some time between the wars by right-wing dictatorships which could be termed fascist. Even stable democracies, such as Great Britain, had fascist parties. One historian has recently calculated that the influence of Fascism affected no fewer than 32 countries in Europe and around the world.

In 1928 Mussolini proudly boasted that Fascism was 'not an article for export'; he believed that he had created something unique in Italy. However, he also announced the complete opposite a few years later when he said that the 20th century would be the century of Fascism and that Italy would be 'the guide for human civilisation'. This sums up the paradox of Fascism which has puzzled and intrigued historians ever since. Can Fascism be satisfactorily defined? If so, was it unique to Mussolini's Italy?

Defining Fascism

A meaningless term?

There are historians who are unwilling to accept the validity of Fascism as a generic term to describe anything other than Mussolini's regime in Italy, for several reasons. The word 'Fascism' is only ever used by the opponents of a party or government – most so-called Fascists regarded their parties as unique. Because Fascism was vague and contradictory in its ideology, satisfactory definition is impossible, since a definition wide enough to include all so-called Fascist regimes would also describe the USSR under Stalin. Finally, the basis of power and the policies followed by each of the regimes described as Fascist were so different that giving them the same label is meaningless.

Common ground: Mussolini and Hitler

Analysis of the rise of Italian Fascism suggests a different conclusion. In particular, a comparison of the way that Mussolini achieved power with Hitler's rise a decade later shows that they had enough in common for the term 'Fascism' to have some meaning and coherence. Both Italy and Germany experienced such deep political and economic problems that democratic government was virtually paralysed. There are also striking parallels between the ideology, tactics and methods used by Mussolini, Hitler and their followers to exploit these problems to their own advantage.

Structural problems in Italy and Germany

Both Italy and Germany were societies in crisis after the First World War, due to a range of similar political, social and economic problems. The Versailles Settlement was bitterly resented by nationalists in both countries, leading to widespread disenchantment with the democratic political system. The postwar period brought further severe economic problems to countries already traumatised by the experience of the First World War. Both Italy and Germany had left-wing movements large enough to pose a threat to the conservative establishment, but not strong enough or united enough actually to take power. Nor were these left-wing parties prepared to form a common front with other parties to fight Fascism. A final factor was the powerful elites, who were happy to see democratic institutions replaced by authoritarian rule, and who believed that they could control fascism to their own advantage.

Fascism and Nazism as political movements

Fascism and Nazism were remarkably similar in their origins, methods and in the kind of people that joined them:

◆ each began as a left-wing movement that drifted to the right, but retained enough of its early socialist ideology to appeal to all social classes;

◆ both regarded themselves as movements, rather than just political parties, open to a wide range of people;

◆ both had a violent paramilitary section, largely recruited from First World War veterans, which dealt ruthlessly with their opponents;

◆ the propaganda methods of both emphasised action not talk, and belief in the cause rather than debate and discussion;

◆ parades, marches, uniforms, rallies and rousing speeches were used to show the power of both movements and create a sense of belonging among the members.

Ideological similarities

Apart from Hitler's emphasis on racism, and especially anti-Semitism, the beliefs of Italian Fascism and German Nazism were almost identical. The core ideas were:

◆ the call for national unity, regeneration and strength;

◆ the need for leadership by a strong, charismatic figure acclaimed (not elected) by his followers;

◆ hatred of the Marxist left – socialists and communists;

◆ dislike of democracy and the values of a liberal, pluralistic society.

Tactics and methods

Mussolini and Hitler were also remarkably similar in the skilful way that each manoeuvred himself into power and retained control of the volatile and fractious movement he led. They faced similar problems and dealt with them in similar ways:

◆ both men had to appear to be respectable and conservative to the elites who held the keys to power;

◆ each had also to stress his revolutionary radicalism to his followers who wanted to destroy the old system;

◆ each was careful not to alienate the Church;

◆ each posed as the only person capable of giving the country strong leadership and controlling the violence of his own followers;

◆ each used the threat of violence as a way of putting pressure on the conservative establishment to allow him into power;

◆ each came to power legally at the head of coalition governments;

◆ each used the legal powers of the state to transform a coalition government into a dictatorship;

◆ each purged the more radical elements of his party once his dictatorship was established.

Although it is impossible to produce an exact and watertight definition of fascism, Mussolini and Hitler had so much in common that it is valid to describe both their regimes as fascist. Furthermore, the common ground between these two regimes and the other right-wing dictatorships of inter-war Europe, such as Franco's Spain, is greater than the differences. It is reasonable to conclude that the rise of Fascism was not just an Italian phenomenon. Mussolini, for all his opportunism, began a movement that had more profound and devastating consequences on the history of Europe and the world in the 20th century than any other.

Further reading

Mussolini has not attracted the same attention from scholars and the general public as Hitler and there are fewer disputes among historians about his importance and legacy. The best biography in English is by Denis Mack Smith (*Mussolini*, 1981). Christopher Hibbert's biography (*Benito Mussolini, The Rise and Fall of Il Duce*, 1962) is useful but does not devote much attention to his rise to power. RH Collier (*Duce!*, 1971) is aimed at the general reader. DG Williamson (*Mussolini, From Socialist to Fascist*, 1997) offers a clear, accessible account of his career and analyses a number of important historiographical issues.

Two important textbooks which place the rise of Fascism in the context of Italian history are by Martin Clark (*Modern Italy, 1871–1982*, 1984) and Denis Mack Smith (*Modern Italy*, 1997). Three recent books that provide succinct and penetrating analysis are by Martin Blinkhorn (*Mussolini and Fascist Italy*, 1984), Philip Morgan (*Italian Fascism, 1919–1945*, 1995) and John Whittam (*Fascist Italy*, 1995). The most authoritative and detailed study of the rise of Italian Fascism remains that of Adrian Lyttelton (*The Seizure of Power, Fascism in Italy, 1919–1929*, 1973).

The debate about the nature of Fascism and of Mussolini's regime has been tackled by a number of contributions to the sixth form history journals: Modern History Review, History Review and New Perspective. A valuable short analysis of Fascism is provided by RAH Robinson (*Fascism, the International Phenomenon*, 1995) and there are more detailed and wide-ranging surveys by HR Kedward (*Fascism in Western Europe, 1900–45*, 1971), FL Carsten (*The Rise of Fascism*, 1967) and Ernst Nolte (*Three Faces of Fascism*, 1963). Important recent publications include Roger Eatwell (*Fascism, A History*, 1996) Stanley Payne (*A History of Fascism, 1914–45*, 1995) and a set of documents edited by Roger Griffin (*Fascism*, 1995).

Glossary

arditi
'The daring ones' – Italy's black-shirted elite troops in the First World War. Many were unable to adjust to peace-time conditions and became early recruits to Fascism.

biennio rosso
'The two red years' – the period of chaos from the middle of 1919 until mid-1921 when Italy seemed on the verge of a socialist revolution.

braccianti
Landless peasant labourers who worked on the commercial farms of the Po valley.

Cheka
Gangs of thugs led by a former criminal, Amerigo Dumini. They were responsible for the murder of Matteotti.

Confindustria
The national association of Italy's major industrial leaders, which supported Fascism.

Fasci
'Bundles' – the name was first used in Sicily in 1893 and described disparate groups of people who had come together for a single purpose.

Fasci di azione revoluzionaria
Formed in 1914, they agitated for Italy to join the First World War on the side of Britain and France.

Fasci di combattimento
Mussolini's 'action groups ' formed in 1919 which became the basis of his Fascist movement.

imboscati
'Shirkers' – an abusive name given to industrial workers whose strikes for higher wages were resented by peasant conscripts in the army.

latifondi
Large landed estates, mainly in the south, often owned by absentee landlords who rented land to peasant tenants or hired landless labourers.

Mezzogiorno
Literally 'midday' – an imaginary line running across the centre of Italy separating the prosperous north from the impoverished south.

Milizia volontaria per la sicurezza nazionale (MVSN)
A national security militia formed from the squadristi in 1923.

obbligati
The 'share-croppers' of central and northern Italy. They paid rent by giving part of their annual crop to the landowners whose estates they farmed.

OVRA – *Opera Volentaria per la Repressione Antifascista*
a secret police force

ras
The name given to local Fascist leaders.

squadristi
Members of the Fascist squads who used violence to intimidate, silence and even murder their political opponents.

Terre Irredente
The 'unredeemed lands' – Trentino and Trieste – which had remained under Austrian rule even though their populations were largely Italian after unification.

trasformismo
The inclusion of potential opposition parties in coalition governments to 'transform' them into supporters of the political system.

1. Italy's post-war Prime Ministers

October 1917 – June 1919	Vittorio Emanuele Orlando
June 1919 – June 1920	Francesco Nitti
June 1920 – July 1921	Giovanni Giolitti
July 1921 – February 1922	Ivanoe Bonomi
February 1922 – October 1922	Luigi Facta
October 1922 – July 1943	Benito Mussolini

2. Levels of illiteracy in selected Italian provinces (%)

Province	1871	1881	1901	1911
Piedmont (north-west)	42.3	32.3	17.7	11.0
Emilia-Romagna (Po Valley)	71.9	63.5	46.3	32.7
Umbria (central)	80.2	73.7	60.3	48.6
Calabria (south)	87.0	85.0	78.7	69.6
Italy as a whole	68.8	61.9	48.7	37.9

A Guide to Mentoring Sports Coaches

ISBN: 978-1-905540-96-9

First Edition

Author/editor: Bill Galvin

Reviewers/sub-editors: Penny Crisfield, Dave Haskins, Zoe Knowles, Lloyd Readhead and Colin Wilson

Revised Edition

Development editor: Vicki Sutton

Technical editor: Kurt Lindley

Coachwise editorial and design team: Craig Smith and Carl Heath

sports coach UK would like to thank the following individuals for their insightful contribution: Mark Beasley, Angela Farr, Sergio Lara-Bercial, Iain Moir, Mick Owen, David Smyth, Malcolm Sumner and David Walker

While every effort has been made to trace and seek permission from copyright holders, the publishers, Coachwise Ltd, invite any unacknowledged copyright holders to email enquiries@coachwise.ltd.uk

It is the publisher's intent to fully credit any unacknowledged copyright holders at the earliest opportunity.

Cover photograph © Mark Bullimore

Published on behalf of sports coach UK by

sports coach UK

Chelsea Close

Off Amberley Road

Armley

Leeds LS12 4HP

Tel: 0113-274 4802

Fax: 0113-231 9606

Email: coaching@sportsco...

Website: www.sportsco...

Patron: HRH The Princ...

Coachwise Ltd

Chelsea Close

Off Amberley Road

Armley

Leeds LS12 4HP

Tel: 0113-231 1310

Fax: 0113-231 9606

Email: ...ies@coachwise.ltd.uk

...w.coachwise.ltd.uk

Throughout this resource, the pronou... ...le and intended to be inclusive

The term parent... ...categories.

sports coach UK will ensure that it has ... ...ctices are inclusive and equitable.